Summary

The recognition of same-sex marriages generates debate on both the federal and state levels. Either legislatively or judicially, same-sex marriage is legal in seven states. Other states allow civil unions or domestic partnerships, which grant all or part of state-level rights, benefits, and/or responsibilities of marriage. Some states have statutes or constitutional amendments limiting marriage to one man and one woman. These variations raise questions about the validity of such unions outside the contracted jurisdiction and have bearing on the distribution of federal benefits.

The Defense of Marriage Act (DOMA), P.L. 104-199, prohibits federal recognition of same-sex marriages and allows individual states to refuse to recognize such marriages performed in other states. Section 3 of DOMA requires that marriage, for purposes of federal benefit programs, be defined as the union of one man and one woman. Lower courts are starting to address DOMA's constitutionality. On July 8, 2010, a U.S. district court in Massachusetts found Section 3 of DOMA unconstitutional in two companion cases brought by same-sex couples married in Massachusetts. In one case, the court found that DOMA exceeded Congress's power under the Spending Clause and violated the Tenth Amendment. In the other, the court held that Congress's goal of preserving the status quo did not bear a rational relationship to DOMA, and thus violated the Fifth Amendment's Equal Protection Clause. While the government filed a notice of appeal in these cases, it is unclear whether the cases will continue. In February 2011, the U.S. Attorney General submitted a letter to congressional leadership stating that the government will not defend DOMA's constitutionality under certain conditions. The Assistant Attorney General subsequently submitted a letter to the First Circuit stating that the government will cease its defense of Section 3 of DOMA. However, the United States will remain a party to the cases presumably to "provide Congress a full and fair opportunity to participate in the litigation."

Questions regarding same-sex marriages figure prominently in California. After the state supreme court's decision finding that denying same-sex couples the right to marry violated the state constitution, voters approved a constitutional amendment ("Proposition 8") limiting the validity and recognition of "marriages" to heterosexual couples. Subsequent court challenges ensued. On February 7, 2012, a panel of the Ninth Circuit Court of Appeals affirmed a lower court decision finding that Proposition 8 violates both the Equal Protection and Due Process Clauses of the Fourteenth Amendment, inasmuch as voters took away a right from a minority group without justification when they approved Proposition 8. In a matter of first impression, the lower court found that Proposition 8 (1) deprived same-sex couples of the fundamental right to marry under the Due Process Clause and (2) excluded such couples from state-sponsored marriage while allowing heterosexual couples access in violation of the Equal Protection Clause. While the appellate court affirmed the lower court's decision, it did so on much narrower grounds based on historical facts specific to California. As such, it appears that this decision will have little, if any, impact on other jurisdictions. However, the case will likely be appealed to the full Ninth Circuit or directly to the U.S. Supreme Court. It is unclear whether the Court would accept the case for review on the merits, as it pertains to an interpretation of a state constitutional amendment.

This report discusses DOMA and legal challenges to it. It reviews legal principles applied to determine the validity of a marriage contracted in another state and surveys the various approaches employed by states to enable or to prevent same-sex marriage. The report also examines House and Senate resolutions introduced in previous Congresses proposing a constitutional amendment and limiting federal courts' jurisdiction to hear or determine any question pertaining to the interpretation of DOMA.

Contents

Tables

Contacts

Introduction

Massachusetts became the first state to legalize same-sex marriages on May 17, 2004, as a result of a November 2003 decision by the state's highest court that denying gay and lesbian couples the right to marry violated the state's constitution.[1] Similarly, state supreme courts in New Jersey,[2] California,[3] Connecticut,[4] and Iowa[5] found that denying same-sex couples the right to marry violated their state constitutions. In addition, the California, Connecticut, and Iowa courts found that parallel statutory structures, including domestic partnerships and/or civil unions, were not the constitutional equivalent of civil marriage. However, in New Jersey, the court left open the option for the state legislature to provide a parallel statutory structure which would allow same-sex couples to enjoy the same rights, privileges, and burdens as married opposite-sex couples.[6] While the aforementioned states legalized same-sex marriages judicially, on April 7, 2009, Vermont became the first state to legalize same-sex marriages legislatively. State legislators garnered a sufficient number of votes to override the governor's veto. Similarly, governors in Maine,[7] New Hampshire, New York,[8] and Washington[9] signed bills legalizing same-sex marriages.

Currently, federal law does not recognize same-sex marriage, nor does any state law other than those of Vermont, Maine, and New Hampshire affirmatively allow gay or lesbian couples to marry.[10] On the federal level, Congress enacted the Defense of Marriage Act (DOMA) to prohibit recognition of same-sex marriages for purposes of federal enactments. States, such as Alabama,[11] Alaska, Arkansas,[12] Arizona,[13] California,[14] Colorado,[15] Florida,[16] Georgia,[17] Hawaii, Idaho,[18] Kansas,[19] Kentucky,[20] Louisiana,[21] Michigan,[22] Mississippi,[23] Missouri,[24] Montana,[25] Nebraska,[26]

---

[1] *Goodridge v. Dept. of Public Health*, 798 N.E.2d 941 (Mass. 2003).

[2] *Lewis v. Harris*, 908 A.2d 196 (NJ 2006).

[3] *In re Marriage Cases*, 183 P.3d 384 (Ca. 2008).

[4] *Kerrigan v. Commissioner of Public Health*, 957 A.2d. 407 (Conn. 2008).

[5] *Varnum v. Brien*, 763 N.W. 2d 862 (Iowa 2009).

[6] *Lewis v. Harris*, 908 A.2d 196 (NJ 2006).

[7] In November 2009, voters overruled the law.

[8] Effective July 24, 2011.

[9] Effective June 7, 2012.

[10] The District of Columbia also allows same-sex marriages.

[11] Voters approved the constitutional ban on June 6, 2006.

[12] Voters approved the constitutional ban on November 2, 2004.

[13] Voters approved the constitutional ban on November 4, 2008.

[14] Voters approved the constitutional ban on November 4, 2008. This vote appears to overrule the California State Supreme Court's decision in *In re Marriage Cases*, 183 P.3d 384 (Ca. 2008) granting same-sex couples the right to marry. On May 26, 2009, the California Supreme Court found the ban was a permissible and valid amendment under the state's constitution. However, the court unanimously held that the amendment applies prospectively and not retroactively. As such, the court upheld same-sex marriages entered into before the amendment's passage. *Strauss v. Horton*, 207 P.3d 48 (Ca. 2009).

[15] Voters approved the constitutional ban on November 7, 2006.

[16] Voters approved the constitutional ban on November 4, 2008.

[17] Voters approved the constitutional ban on November 2, 2004.

[18] Voters approved the constitutional ban on November 7, 2006.

[19] Voters approved the constitutional ban on April 5, 2005.

[20] Voters approved the constitutional ban on November 2, 2004.

Nevada, North Carolina,[27] North Dakota,[28] Ohio,[29] Oklahoma,[30] Oregon,[31] South Carolina,[32] South Dakota,[33] Tennessee,[34] Texas,[35] Utah, Virginia,[36] and Wisconsin[37] have enacted state constitutional amendments limiting marriage to one man and one woman. Seventeen other states have enacted statutes limiting marriage in some manner.[38] **Table 1** summarizes these various approaches.

(...continued)

[21] Voters approved the constitutional ban on September 18, 2004. The Louisiana Supreme Court reversed a state district judge's ruling striking down the amendment on the grounds that it violated a provision of the state constitution requiring that an amendment cover only one subject. The Court found that each provision of the amendment is germane to the single object of defense of marriage and constitutes an element of the plan advanced to achieve this object. *Forum for Equality PAC v. McKeithen*, 893 So.3d 715 (La. 2005). Similarly, the Georgia Supreme Court reversed a lower court's ruling. *Perdue v. O'Kelley*, 280 GA 732 (GA. 2006). Other states that also have single-subject requirements, Ohio and Oklahoma, may face similar legal challenges.

[22] Voters approved the constitutional ban on November 2, 2004.

[23] Voters approved the constitutional ban on November 2, 2004.

[24] Voters approved the constitutional ban on August 3, 2004.

[25] Voters approved the constitutional ban on November 2, 2004.

[26] A U.S. district court judge struck down Nebraska's ban on gay marriage, saying that the ban "imposes significant burdens on both the expressive and intimate associational rights" of gays "and creates a significant barrier to the plaintiffs' right to petition or to participate in the political process." *Citizens for Equal Protection Inc., v. Bruning*, 368 F.Supp.2d 980 (D. NE May 12, 2005). However, the Eighth Circuit Court of Appeals reversed finding that the Nebraska's constitutional amendment "and other laws limiting the state-recognized institution of marriage to heterosexual couples are rationally related to legitimate state interest and therefore do not violate the Constitution of the United States." *Citizens for Equal Protection Inc., v. Bruning*, 455 F.3d 859 (8th Cir. 2006).

[27] Voters approved the constitutional ban on May 8, 2012.

[28] Voters approved the constitutional ban on November 2, 2004.

[29] Voters approved the constitutional ban on November 2, 2004.

[30] Voters approved the constitutional ban on November 2, 2004.

[31] Voters approved the constitutional ban on November 2, 2004. On April 4, 2005, the Oregon Supreme Court invalidated Multnomah County same-sex marriages, stating that the marriage licenses were issued to same-sex couples without authority and were void at the time they were issued. *Li v. State*, 110 P.3d 91 (Or. 2005).

[32] Voters approved the constitutional ban on November 7, 2006.

[33] Voters approved the constitutional ban on November 7, 2006.

[34] Voters approved the constitutional ban on November 7, 2006.

[35] Voters approved the constitutional ban on November 8, 2005.

[36] Voters approved the constitutional ban on November 7, 2006.

[37] Voters approved the constitutional ban on November 7, 2006.

[38] These states are Arizona, California, Delaware, Florida, Illinois, Indiana, Iowa, Maine, Maryland, Minnesota, New Hampshire, North Carolina, Pennsylvania, Vermont, Washington, West Virginia, and Wyoming.

Defense of Marriage Act (DOMA)[39]

In 1996, Congress approved the DOMA "[t]o define and protect the institution of marriage." It allows all states, territories, possessions, and Indian tribes to refuse to recognize an act of any other jurisdiction that designates a relationship between individuals of the same sex as a marriage. Section 2 of DOMA states:

> No State, territory, or possession of the United States, or Indian tribe, shall be required to give effect to any public act, record, or judicial proceeding of any other State, territory, possession, or tribe respecting a relationship between persons of the same sex that is treated as a marriage under the laws of such other State, territory, possession, or tribe, or a right or claim arising from such relationship.[40]

Furthermore, Section 3 of DOMA goes on to declare that the terms "marriage" and "spouse," as used in federal enactments, exclude same-sex marriage.

> In determining the meaning of any Act of Congress, or of any ruling, regulation, or interpretation of the various administrative bureaus and agencies of the United States, the word "marriage" means only a legal union between one man and one woman as husband and wife, and the word "spouse" refers only to a person of the opposite sex who is a husband or a wife.[41]

---

[39] P.L. 104-199, 110 Stat. 2419 (codified at 1 U.S.C. §7 and 28 U.S.C. §1738C).

[40] 28 U.S.C. §1738C.

[41] 1 U.S.C. §7.

Constitutional Challenges to DOMA in Federal Courts[42]

As federal agencies grapple with the interplay of DOMA and the distribution of federal marriage-based benefits, lower courts are beginning to address the DOMA's constitutionality and the appropriate standard (strict, intermediate, or rational basis) of review. Plaintiffs and legal scholars have argued that the DOMA is an unconstitutional exercise of Congress's authority under its Spending Power and Full Faith and Credit Clauses of the U.S. Constitution. In two cases within the First Circuit a federal district court found DOMA unconstitutional under the Tenth Amendment and the Equal Protection Clause of the Fifth Amendment. Two cases are pending in the Second Circuit. On February 23, 2011, the Attorney General sent a letter to the congressional leadership informing it that the Department of Justice (DOJ) will not defend DOMA's constitutionality in these cases. It is unclear what impact, if any, the Attorney General's letter will have on other pending litigation.

---

[42] It should be noted that a federal bankruptcy court in the Central District of California found DOMA unconstitutional. Two male debtors, legally married in California, filed a joint bankruptcy petition. The U.S. Trustee sought to dismiss the joint petition because the debtors are two males. In denying the Trustee's motion, the court found DOMA violates the Equal Protection Clause of the Fifth Amendment under either a heightened scrutiny or rational basis analysis. *In re Balas*, 2011 WL 2312169 (Bankr. C.D. Cal. June 13, 2011) (No. 2:11-BK-17831 TD). Bankruptcy courts in other jurisdictions have also allowed joint bankruptcy petitions for same-sex couples without reaching a conclusion on DOMA's constitutionality. *See, e.g., In re Somers*, 448 B.R. 677 (Bankr. S.D.N.Y., 2011 No. 10-38296). However, in an earlier case, the federal bankruptcy court in the Western District of Washington found DOMA constitutional. Two American women, married in British Columbia, Canada filed a joint bankruptcy petition in Tacoma, challenging the definitional part of DOMA. The court ruled that there was no fundamental constitutional right to marry someone of the same sex and that DOMA did not violate the Fourth, Fifth or Tenth amendments, nor the principles of comity. *In re Lee Kandu and Ann C. Kandu*, 315 B.R. 123 (Bankr. W.D. Wash, 2004 No. 03-51312). These decisions are not binding on other courts.

In *Wilson v. Ake*, a same-sex couple sought a declaration that their marriage was valid for federal and Florida law purposes. To issue such a declaration, the court would have had to invalidate both the federal DOMA and the Florida statutes defining marriage the same way and expressly forbidding courts to recognize same-sex marriages from other states. The *Wilson* court declined to invalidate any of the relevant statutes finding that (1) DOMA did not violate the Full Faith and Credit Clause; (2) the right to marry a person of the same sex was not a fundamental right guaranteed by the Due Process Clause; (3) homosexuals were not a suspect class warranting strict scrutiny of equal protection claim; (4) under a rational basis analysis, DOMA did not violate equal protection or due process guarantees; and (5) the Florida statute prohibiting same-sex marriage is constitutional. *Wilson v. Ake*, 354 F.Supp.3d 1298 (M.D. Florida 2005). Moreover, the *Wilson* court found that it was bound by the U.S. Supreme Court's decision in *Baker v. Nelson*, 191 N.W.2d 185 (1971), *appeal dismissed*, 409 U.S. 810 (1972).

In *Baker v. Nelson*, two adult males' application for a marriage license was denied by the county clerk because the petitioners were of the same sex. The plaintiffs appealed to the Minnesota Supreme Court. Plaintiffs argued that Minnesota Statute §517.08, which did not authorize marriage between persons of the same sex, violated the First, Eighth, Ninth and Fourteenth Amendments of the U.S. Constitution. The Minnesota Supreme Court rejected plaintiffs' assertion that "the right to marry without regard to the sex of the parties is a fundamental right of all persons" and held that §517.08 did not violate the Due Process Clause or Equal Protection Clause. 191 N.W.2d at 186-87.

The plaintiffs appealed the Minnesota Supreme Court's ruling to the U.S. Supreme Court pursuant to 28 U.S.C. §1257(2). Under 28 U.S.C. §1257, the Supreme Court has discretion to refuse to adjudicate the case on its merits. The Supreme Court ultimately dismissed the appeal "for want of a substantial federal question." *Baker*, 409 U.S. at 810.

The *Wilson* court, relying on *Hicks v. Miranda* (422 U.S. 332 [1975]), found that a dismissal for lack of a substantial federal question constitutes an adjudication on the merits that is binding on lower federal courts.

Full Faith and Credit Clause

Some argue that DOMA is an unconstitutional exercise of Congress's authority under the Full Faith and Credit Clause of the U.S. Constitution,[43] which states: "Full Faith and Credit shall be given in each State to the public Acts, Records, and judicial Proceedings of every other State; And the Congress may by general Laws prescribe the Manner in which such Acts, Records and Proceedings shall be proved, and the Effect thereof."

Opponents argue that, although Congress has authority to pass laws that enable acts, judgments, and the like to be given effect in other states, it has no constitutional power to pass a law permitting states to deny full faith and credit to another state's laws and judgments.[44] Conversely, some argue that DOMA does nothing more than simply restate the power granted to the states by the Full Faith and Credit Clause.[45] While there is no judicial precedent on this issue, Congress's general authority to "prescribe ... the effect" of public acts arguably gives it discretion to define the "effect" so that a particular public act is not due full faith and credit. Thus, plain reading of the clause appears to encompass both expansion and contraction.[46]

Equal Protection[47]

Congress's authority to legislate in this manner under the Full Faith and Credit Clause, if the analysis set out above is accepted, does not conclude the matter. There are multiple constitutional constraints upon federal legislation. One that is relevant is the Equal Protection Clause in the Fourteenth Amendment and the effect of the Supreme Court's decision in *Romer v. Evans*,[48] which struck down a referendum-adopted provision of the Colorado Constitution, which repealed local ordinances that provided civil-rights protections for gay persons and which prohibited all governmental action designed to protect gays and lesbians from discrimination. The Court held that, under the Equal Protection Clause, legislation adverse to homosexuals was to be scrutinized under a "rational basis" standard of review.[49] The classification failed to pass even this deferential standard of review, because it imposed a special disability on homosexuals not visited on any other class of people and it could not be justified by any of the arguments made by the state. The state argued that its purpose for the amendment was two-fold: (1) to respect the freedom of association rights of other citizens, such as landlords and employers who objected to

---

[43] U.S. Const. Art. IV, §1.

[44] See 142 Cong. Rec. S5931-33 (June 6, 1996) (statement introducing Professor Laurence H. Tribe's letter into the record concluding that DOMA "would be an unconstitutional attempt by Congress to limit the full faith and credit clause of the Constitution.").

[45] See Paige E. Chabora, Congress' Power Under the Full Faith and Credit Clause and the Defense of Marriage Act of 1996, 76 Neb. L. Rev. 604, 621-35 (1997).

[46] *See, e.g., Wilson v. Ake*, 354 F.Supp.2d at 1302 (finding that DOMA was an appropriate exercise of Congress's power to regulate conflicts between the laws of different states, and holding otherwise would create "a license for a single State to create national policy.").

[47] The Fifth Amendment applies to the federal government while the Fourteenth Amendment applies to the states. In *Bolling v. Sharpe* (347 U.S. 497 [1954]), the U.S. Supreme Court interpreted the Fifth Amendment's Due Process Clause to include an equal protection element. In Buckley v. Valeo (424 U.S. 1, 93 [1976]), the Court stated that "[e]qual protection analysis in the Fifth Amendment area, is the same as that under the Fourteenth Amendment."

[48] 517 U.S. 620 (1996).

[49] *Id.*

---

homosexuality; and (2) to serve the state's interest in conserving resources to fight discrimination against other protected groups.

DOMA can be distinguished from the Colorado amendment. DOMA's legislative history indicates that it was intended to protect federalism interests and state sovereignty in the area of domestic relations, historically a subject of almost exclusive state concern. Moreover, it permits but does not require states to deny recognition to same-sex marriages in other states, affording states with strong public policy concerns the discretion to effectuate that policy. Thus, it can be argued that DOMA is grounded not in hostility to homosexuals but in an intent to afford the states the discretion to act as their public policy on same-sex marriage dictates.

In *Gill v. Office of Personnel Management*,[50] a U.S. District Court in Massachusetts found that Section 3 of DOMA, which defines the terms "marriage" and "spouse" to exclude same-sex marriages, failed to pass constitutional muster under the highly deferential rational basis analysis.[51] In this case, same-sex couples married in Massachusetts challenged DOMA alleging that they were denied certain federal marriage-based benefits available to similarly situated heterosexual couples. The benefits sought encompassed three programs: the Federal Employees Health Benefits Program (FEHB), the Federal Employees Dental and Vision Insurance Program (FEDVIP), and the federal Flexible Spending Account Program.

In reaching its decision, the court looked to the DOMA's legislative history, which identified four interests that Congress sought to advance in the law's enactment: (1) encouraging responsible procreation and child-bearing, (2) defending and nurturing the institution of traditional heterosexual marriage, (3) defending traditional notions of morality, and (4) preserving scarce resources.[52] The court found that these interests do not bear a rational basis upon which to exclude same-sex marriages from federal recognition as procreation is not a precondition of marriage.[53] Nor does the non-recognition of same-sex marriages encourage such individuals to marry opposite-sex partners or strengthen heterosexual marriages. According to the court, "mere negative attitudes, or fear, unsubstantiated by factors which are properly cognizable [by the government] are decidedly impermissible basis upon which to ground a legislative classification."[54]

The government proffered additional arguments which the court discounted. The court found that there was no interest in providing a uniform definition of marriage for purposes of determining federal rights. The court noted that the federal government has "fully embraced" the myriad of state marriage laws by "recognizing as valid for federal purposes any heterosexual marriage which has been declared valid pursuant to state law."[55] The court found persuasive the fact that the DOMA represented the first time that the federal government attempted to mandate a uniform definition of marriage. As in *Romer*, the district court concluded that the absence of precedent for this legislative classification demonstrated a hostility toward same-sex couples. And animus alone is not a legitimate basis for the government to act.[56] In addition, the court concluded that "there

---

[50] 699 F.Supp. 2d 374 (D. Mass. 2010).

[51] The court declined to address whether classification based on sexual orientation warrants heightened scrutiny.

[52] H.R. Rep. 104-664, 104th Cong., 2d Sess. 12-18.

[53] 699 F.Supp. 2d 374.

[54] *Id.* at 389.

[55] *Id.* at 390.

[56] *Id.* at 396.

---

exists no fairly conceivable set of facts that could ground a rational relationship between DOMA and a legitimate government objective."[57]

Substantive Due Process (Right to Privacy)

Another potential constitutional constraint is the Due Process Clause of the Fourteenth Amendment and the effect of the Supreme Court's decision in *Lawrence v. Texas*,[58] which struck down under the Due Process Clause a state statute criminalizing certain private sexual acts between homosexuals. The Court held that the Fourteenth Amendment's Due Process privacy guarantee extends to protect consensual sex between adult homosexuals. The Court noted that the Due Process right to privacy protects certain personal decisions from governmental interference. These personal decisions include issues regarding contraceptives, abortion, marriage, procreation, and family relations.[59] The Court extended this right to privacy to cover adult consensual homosexual sodomy.

It is currently unclear what impact, if any, the Court's decision in *Lawrence* will have on legal challenges to laws prohibiting same-sex marriage. On the one hand, this decision can be viewed as affirming a broad constitutional right to sexual privacy. Conversely, the Court distinguished this case from cases involving minors and "whether the government must give formal recognition to any relationship that homosexual persons seek to enter."[60] Courts may seek to distinguish statutes prohibiting same-sex marriage from statutes criminalizing homosexual conduct. Courts may view the preservation of the institution of marriage as sufficient justification for statutes banning same-sex marriage. Moreover, courts may view the public recognition of marriage differently than the sexual conduct of homosexuals in the privacy of their own homes.[61]

Tenth Amendment and Spending Power

Another potential constitutional constraint is the Tenth Amendment coupled with the Spending Clause of the U.S. Constitution. Article I, Section 8, of the Constitution limits congressional authority to act by specifying general subject categories where federal action is permissible. Under this section and the Tenth Amendment,[62] categories other than those enumerated in Section 8 or elsewhere are reserved for state action. Enumerated powers encompass those topics the Constitution's framers thought could be best handled on the national level; for example, waging war, national defense, interstate and foreign commerce, coinage and currency, the postal system, bankruptcies, copyrights, and the federal judicial system. Generally, family law issues, including

---

[57] *Id.* at 387. It is unclear whether the government will appeal the decision.

[58] 539 U.S. 558 (2003). For a legal analysis of this decision, refer to CRS Report RL31681, *Homosexuality and the Constitution: A Legal Analysis of the Supreme Court Ruling in Lawrence v. Texas*, by Jody Feder.

[59] *Lawrence v. Texas*, 539 U.S. 558 (2003).

[60] *Id.* at 2484. *See, e.g., Wilson v. Ake*, 354 F.Supp.2d at 1306 (declining to interpret *Lawrence* as creating a fundamental right to same-sex marriage).

[61] As the discussion of state courts' reasoning on this issue, discussed below, indicates, state constitutions—not the U.S. Constitution—are generally the source of interpreting laws governing marriage. To date, only the Arizona Court of Appeals has considered the impact of *Lawrence*. Even then, it did not interpret the case as proscribing state law banning same-sex marriage.

[62] The Tenth Amendment provides that "powers not delegated to the United States by the Constitution, nor prohibited by it to the States, are reserved to the States respectively, or to the people."

"declarations of status, e.g., marriage, annulment, divorce, custody and paternity,"[63] are deemed to fall within a state's purview.[64]

In instances where Congress lacks a direct justification for federal legislation, it often relies on its enumerated spending power. Article I, Section 8, clause I empowers Congress "to lay and collect Taxes … to provide for the … general Welfare." There is a general consensus that Congress has expansive powers to attach conditions to grants of federal money, including grants to states. In *South Dakota v. Dole*,[65] the Supreme Court considered a federal law that required the Secretary of Transportation to withhold 5% of a state's federal highway dollars if the state allowed persons under 21 years of age to purchase alcoholic beverages. South Dakota, which allowed 18-year-olds to make such purchases and was in a position to lose federal funds for highway construction, sued, arguing that the highway funding law was unrelated to setting a national drinking age. In upholding the federal law, the Court announced a four-part test to evaluate the constitutionality of conditions attached to federal spending programs: (1) the spending power must be exercised in pursuit of the general welfare, (2) the grant conditions must be clearly stated, (3) the conditions must be related to a federal interest in the national program or project, and (4) the spending power cannot be used to induce states to do things that would themselves be unconstitutional.[66]

In *Massachusetts v. U.S. Dept. of Health and Human Services*,[67] a federal district court found that DOMA exceeded Congress's power under the Spending Clause and violated the Tenth Amendment. Specifically, the court found that DOMA imposes an unconstitutional condition on the receipt of federal funding and intrudes on an "attribute of state sovereignty"—namely the regulation of marital status. Massachusetts challenged DOMA's constitutionality where the U.S. Department of Veterans Affairs (VA) informed the Commonwealth's Department of Veterans' Services that the federal government was entitled to recapture grant money if the Commonwealth entombed same-sex spouses of veterans at two state veterans' cemeteries (owned and operated solely by the Commonwealth).

In finding that Congress exceeded the scope of its authority by enacting DOMA, the district court first found that DOMA violates the Equal Protection Clause of the Fifth Amendment. As in its companion case (*Gill v. Office of Personnel Management*), the court found that DOMA failed to pass constitutional muster under the highly deferential rational basis analysis. Additionally, the court concluded that "DOMA plainly conditions the receipt of federal funding on the denial of marriage-based benefits to same-sex married couples, though the same benefits are provided to similarly-situated heterosexual couples."[68] Accordingly, the court found that such an action exceeds Congress's authority under its spending power.[69]

---

[63] *Ankenbrandt v. Richards*, 504 U.S. 689 (1992)(Blackmun, J., concurring).

[64] *See, e.g., Boggs v. Boggs*, 520 U.S. 833, 848 (1997)(stating that "[a]s a general matter, '[t]he whole subject of the domestic relations of husband and wife, parent and child, belongs to the laws of the States and not to the laws of the United States.'"); *Haddock v. Haddock*, 201 U.S. 562 (1906)(stating that "[n]o one denies that the States, at the time of the adoption of the Constitution, possessed full power over the subject of marriage and divorce [and that] the Constitution delegated no authority to the Government of the United States on [that subject].").

[65] 483 U.S. 203 (1987).

[66] *Id.* at 207-11.

[67] 698 F. Supp. 2d 235 (D. Mass. 2010).

[68] *Id.* at 348.

[69] *Id.*

U.S. Department of Justice Statement and Letter on Litigation Involving the Constitutionality of DOMA

While the government had filed a notice of appeal in the Massachusetts cases, it is unclear whether these cases will proceed. On February 23, 2011, the U.S. Attorney General sent a letter to congressional leadership informing it that the department will not defend the constitutionality of Section 3 of DOMA (which for federal benefits defines the term "marriage" and "spouse" to exclude same-sex marriages) under certain circumstances. Under an equal protection challenge to Section 3 of DOMA, a court must first determine the appropriate standard of review. Based on several factors, the President and the Attorney General have concluded that the appropriate review for such a challenge should be "heightened scrutiny" and that the section as applied to same-sex marriages fails to meet that standard. The letter specifically addresses two cases pending in district court in the Second Circuit (*Windsor v. United States*, No. 1:10-cv-8435 [(S.D.N.Y]) and *Pedersen v. OPM*, No. 3:10-cv-1750 [D.Conn.]), where there is no binding precedent on the appropriate review for classifications based on "sexual orientation."[70] Specifically, the Attorney General stated:

> I will instruct the Department's lawyers to immediately inform the district courts in *Windsor* and *Pederson* of the Executive Branch's view that heightened scrutiny is the appropriate standard of review and that, consistent with that standard, Section 3 of DOMA may not be constitutionally applied to same-sex couples whose marriages are legally recognized under state law.

While the department will not defend the constitutionality of Section 3 of DOMA in the named Second Circuit cases, it will remain a party to them and "continue to represent the interests of the United States throughout the litigation" presumably to allow "Members who wish to defend the statute [to] pursue that option."[71] It is important to note that the executive branch will continue to comply with Section 3 of DOMA in disbursing federal benefits. Specifically, the Attorney General's letter states:

> Notwithstanding this determination, the President has informed me that Section 3 will continue to be enforced by the Executive Branch. To that end, the President has instructed Executive agencies to continue to comply with Section 3 of DOMA, consistent with the Executive's obligation to take care that the laws be faithfully executed, unless and until Congress repeals Section 3 or the judicial branch renders a definitive verdict against the law's constitutionality.

The Attorney General states further:

> Furthermore, pursuant to the President's instructions, and upon further notification to Congress, I will instruct Department attorneys to advise courts in other pending DOMA litigation of the President's and my conclusions that a heightened standard should apply, that Section 3 is unconstitutional under that standard and that the Department will cease defense of Section 3.

---

[70] U.S. Department of Justice, "Letter From Attorney General to Congress on Litigation Involving the Defense of Marriage Act," February 23, 2011, located at http://www.justice.gov/opa/pr/2011/February/11-ag-223 html (last accessed February 28, 2011).

[71] U.S. Department of Justice, "Statement of the Attorney General on Litigation Involving the Defense of Marriage Act," press release, February 23, 2011, located at http://www.justice.gov/opa/pr/2011/February/11-ag-223 html (last accessed February 28, 2011).

On February 24, 2011, the Assistant Attorney General submitted a similar letter to the First Circuit indicating that it will "cease its defense of Section 3."[72] It is unclear as to whether the department will continue to defend DOMA's constitutionality against other challenges including the Tenth Amendment/Spending Power (as in *Massachusetts v. U.S. Dept. of Health and Human Services*)[73] or any cases employing a rational basis analysis (as in *Gill v. Office of Personnel Management*).[74]

Interstate Recognition of Marriage

DOMA opponents take the position that the Full Faith and Credit Clause would obligate states to recognize same-sex marriages contracted in other states in which they are authorized. This conclusion is far from evident as this clause applies principally to the interstate recognition and enforcement of judgments.[75] It is settled law that final judgments are entitled to full faith and credit, regardless of other states' public policies, provided the issuing state had jurisdiction over the parties and the subject matter.[76] The Full Faith and Credit Clause has rarely been used by courts to validate marriages because marriages are not "legal judgments."

Questions concerning the validity of an out-of-state marriage are generally resolved without reference to the Full Faith and Credit Clause. In the legal sense, marriage is a "civil contract" created by the state which establishes certain duties and confers certain benefits.[77] Validly entering the contract creates the marital status; the duties and benefits attached by a state are incidents of that status. As such, the general tendency, based on comity rather than on compulsion under the Full Faith and Credit Clause, is to recognize marriages contracted in other states even if they could not have been celebrated in the recognizing state.

The general rule of validation for marriage is to look to the law of the place where the marriage was celebrated. A marriage satisfying the contracting state's requirements will usually be held valid everywhere.[78] Many states provide by statute that a marriage that is valid where contracted is valid within the state. This "place of celebration" rule is then subject to a number of exceptions, most of which are narrowly construed. The most common exception to the "place of celebration" rule is for marriages deemed contrary to the forum's strong public policy. Several states, such as Connecticut,[79] Idaho,[80] Illinois,[81] Kansas,[82] Missouri,[83] Pennsylvania,[84] South Carolina,[85] and

---

[72] Letter from Tony Wes, Assistant Attorney General, to Margaret Carter, Clerk of the U.S. Court of Appeals for the First Circuit (February 24, 2011) found at http://metroweekly.com/poliglot/doj-letter-re-ma-doma-cases-02-2011.pdf, last accessed March 7, 2011.

[73] 698 F.Supp.2d 235 (D. Mass. 2010).

[74] 699 F.Supp. 2d 374 (D. Mass. 2010).

[75] See H.Rept. 104-664, 1996 U.S.C.C.A.N. 2905 (stating that "marriage licensure is not a judgment"). See also, 28 U.S.C. §1738 (defining which acts, records and judicial proceedings are afforded full faith and credit).

[76] *Restatement (Second) of Conflict of Laws* §107.

[77] On the state level, common examples of nonnegotiable marital rights and obligations include distinct income tax filing status; public assistance such as health and welfare benefits; default rules concerning community property distribution and control; dower, curtesy and inheritance rights; child custody, child agreements; name change rights; spouse and marital communications privileges in legal proceedings; and the right to bring wrongful death, and other legal actions.

[78] See 2 Restatement (Second) of Conflict of Laws §283.

[79] Conn. Gen Stat. Ann. §45a-803-4.

[80] Idaho Code §32-209.

Tennessee,[86] provide an exception to this general rule by declaring out-of-state marriages void if against the state's public policy or if entered into with the intent to evade the law of the state. This exception applies only where another state's law violates "some fundamental principle of justice, some prevalent conception of good morals, some deep-rooted tradition of the common weal."[87]

Section 283 of the Restatement (Second) of Law provides:

> (1) The validity of marriage will be determined by the local law of the state which, with respect to the particular issue, has the most significant relationship to the spouses and the marriage under the principles stated in §6.

> (2) A marriage which satisfies the requirements of the state where the marriage was contracted will everywhere be recognized as valid unless it violates the strong public policy of another state which had the most significant relationship to the spouses and the marriage at the time of the marriage.

Same-Sex Marriage Activity in the States

State Litigation

Massachusetts

Massachusetts, unlike 26 states and the federal government, has not adopted a "defense of marriage statute" defining marriage as a union between a man and woman.[88] On April 11, 2001, a Boston-based homosexual rights group, Gay and Lesbian Advocates and Defenders (GLAD), filed suit against the Massachusetts Department of Public Health on behalf of seven same-sex couples. The plaintiffs claimed that "refusing same-sex couples the opportunity to apply for a marriage license" violates Massachusetts's law and various portions of the Massachusetts Constitution. GLAD's brief argued the existence of a fundamental right to marry "the person of one's choosing" in the due process provisions of the Massachusetts Constitution and asserted that the marriage laws, which allow both men and women to marry, violate equal protection provisions.[89]

(...continued)

[81] 750 Ill. Comp. Stat. 5/201.

[82] Kan. Stat. Ann. §23-101.

[83] Mo. Rev. Stat. §451.022.

[84] Pa. Stat. Ann. tit. 23 §1704.

[85] S.C. Code Ann. §20-1-10.

[86] Tenn. Code Ann. §36-3-113.

[87] *Loucks v. Standard Oil Co.*, 120 N.E. 198, 202 (N.Y. 1918)(defining public policy as a valid reason for closing the forum to suit); *see, e.g., Shea v. Shea*, 63 N.E.2d 113 (N.Y. 1945)(finding that a common law marriage validly contracted in another state should not be recognized in New York, where common law marriage was prohibited by statute).

[88] It should be noted that, prior to the *Goodridge* case, in *Adoption of Tammy*, 619 N.E. 2d 315 (Mass. 1993), the Supreme Judicial Court had interpreted "marriage" to mean "the union of one man and one woman."

[89] *Hillary Goodridge v. Dept. of Public Health*, 14 Mass. L. Rptr. 591 (Suffolk County, Super. Ct. May 7, 2002).

The Superior Court rejected the plaintiffs' arguments after exploring the application of the word marriage, the construction of marriage statutes, and finally, the historical purpose of marriage. The trial court found that based on history and the actions of the people's elected representatives, a right to same-sex marriage was not so rooted in tradition that a failure to recognize it violated fundamental liberty, nor was it implicit in ordered liberty.[90] Moreover, the court held that in excluding same-sex couples from marriage, the Commonwealth did not deprive them of substantive due process, liberty, or freedom of speech or association.[91] The court went on to find that limiting marriage to opposite-sex couples was rationally related to a legitimate state interest in encouraging procreation.[92]

On November 18, 2003, the Massachusetts Supreme Judicial Court overruled the lower court and held that, under the Massachusetts Constitution, the Commonwealth could not deny the protections, benefits, and obligations attendant on marriage to two individuals of the same sex who wish to marry.[93] The court concluded that interpreting the statutory term "marriage" to apply only to male-female unions lacked a rational basis for either due process or equal protection purposes under the state's constitution. Moreover, the court found that such a limitation was not justified by the state's interest in providing a favorable setting for procreation and had no rational relationship to the state's interests in ensuring that children be raised in optimal settings and in conservation of state and private financial resources.[94] The court reasoned that the laws of civil marriage did not privilege procreative heterosexual intercourse, nor contain any requirement that applicants for marriage licenses attest to their ability or intention to conceive children by coitus. Moreover, the court reasoned that the state has no power to provide varying levels of protection to children based on the circumstances of birth. As for the state's interest in conserving scarce state and private financial resources, the court found that the state failed to produce any evidence to support its assertion that same-sex couples were less financially interdependent than opposite-sex couples. In addition, Massachusetts marriage laws do not condition receipt of public and private financial benefits to married individuals on a demonstration of financial dependence on each other.[95] As this decision is based on the Commonwealth's constitution, it is not reviewable by the U.S. Supreme Court. The court stayed its decision for 180 days to give the legislature time to enact legislation "as it may deem appropriate in light of this opinion."[96]

On February 3, 2004, the court ruled, in an advisory opinion to the state senate, that civil unions are not the constitutional equivalent of civil marriage.[97] The court reasoned that the establishment of civil unions for same-sex couples would create a separate class of citizens by status discrimination which would violate the equal protection and due process requirements of the Constitution of the Commonwealth.[98]

---

[90] *Id.*

[91] *Id.*

[92] *Id.*

[93] *Hillary Goodridge v. Dept. of Public Health*, 798 N.E.2d 941 (Mass. 2003).

[94] *Id.* at 964 (stating that it "cannot be rational under our laws, and indeed is not permitted, to penalize children by depriving them of state benefits because the state disapproves of their parents' sexual orientation.")

[95] *Id.* at 965.

[96] *Id.* at 968.

[97] The state Senate asked the court whether it would be sufficient for the legislature to pass a law allowing same-sex civil unions that would confer "all of the benefits, protections, rights and responsibilities of marriage."

[98] Opinions of the Justices to the Senate, SJC-01963, 802 N.E.2d 565 (Mass. 2004).

"Marriage" Versus Domestic Partnership or Civil Union: Standards of Review

In the years following the Massachusetts decision, state supreme courts in New Jersey, California, Connecticut, and Iowa addressed the issue of same-sex marriage.[99] The California and Connecticut cases posed a slightly different question than the one presented in Massachusetts and Iowa, as California and Connecticut legislatures enacted parallel statutory schemes in the form of domestic partnerships and civil unions granting the states' same-sex couples the same rights and benefits as well as the obligations of civil marriage. As such, the legal issue before the California and Connecticut supreme courts was whether, in light of both marriage and domestic partnership/civil union statutes, the failure to designate the official relationship of same-sex couples as marriage violates the states' constitutions.[100] Likewise, courts in Connecticut and Iowa found that civil unions are not equivalent to marriage.

California

While the California Supreme Court held that the privacy, due process, and equal protection provisions of the state's constitution guarantee the basic right of civil marriage to all individuals and couples regardless of their sexual orientation,[101] the Connecticut and Iowa supreme courts focused on the equal protection provision of their state constitutions.[102] In addressing the privacy and due process challenges, the California majority first looked at the nature and scope of the "right to marry." Relying on judicial precedent and legislative history,[103] the court concluded that the fundamental nature of the substantive rights embodied in the right to marry, and their central importance to one's opportunity to live a happy, meaningful, and satisfying life as a full member of society, require that the state constitution be interpreted to protect this right not to be "eliminated or abrogated by the Legislature or by the electorate through the statutory initiative process."[104] In reaching its conclusion, the court discussed the societal benefits of marriage, including child welfare and the role that marriage plays in "facilitating a stable family setting."[105] Furthermore, the court described marriage as the "basic unit" or "building block" of society.[106] The court noted that while marriage serves a vital societal interest, judicial precedent also demonstrated that the right to marry is an "integral component of an individual's interest in personal autonomy" protected by the privacy and liberty interest provisions of the California constitution.[107]

---

[99] As these decisions are based exclusively on state constitutional provisions, they are non-reviewable by the United States Supreme Court.

[100] See, *Kerrigan v. Commissioner of Public Health*, 957 A.2d 407, 412 (Conn. 2008)(stating "... because the institution of marriage carries with it a status and significance that the newly created classification of civil unions does not embody, the segregation of heterosexual and homosexual couples into separate institutions constitutes a cognizable harm.").

[101] *In re Marriage Cases*, 183 P.3d 384 (2008).

[102] *Kerrigan v. Commissioner of Public Health*, 957 A.2d 407 (Conn. 2008); *Varnum v. Brien*, 763 N.W. 2d 862 (Iowa 2009)(stating "... a new distinction based on sexual orientation would be equally suspect and difficult to square with the fundamental principles of equal protection embodied in our constitution.").

[103] *See,* 183 P.3d 384, 407-410 (discussing the legislative history of marriage statutes).

[104] *Id.* at 399.

[105] *Id.* at 423.

[106] *Id.*

[107] *Id.*

While the California court acknowledged that the constitutional right to marry did not obligate the state to afford specific tax or other governmental benefits on the basis of a couple's family relation, the right to marry does "obligate the state to take affirmative action to grant official, public recognition to the couple's relationship as a family."[108] Thus, the court concluded that the California constitution guarantees same-sex couples the same "substantive constitutional rights as opposite-sex couples to choose one's life partner and enter with that person in a committed, officially recognized, and protected family relationship that enjoys all of the constitutionally based incidents of marriage."[109]

In addressing the equal protection question, the California Supreme Court used a different standard of review than the Connecticut and Iowa supreme courts. In a matter of first impression, the California Supreme Court determined that strict scrutiny was the appropriate standard of review for sexual orientation discrimination. According to the California court, classification or discrimination on the basis of sexual orientation is analogous to race, gender,[110] or religious discrimination, as these types of classifications are based on characteristics that bear no relationship to one's ability to perform or contribute to society.[111] As such, the California court expanded protection against sexual orientation discrimination by determining that strict scrutiny was the appropriate review.

Under the heightened standard of strict scrutiny, the state had to establish (1) a compelling state interest, and (2) that the differential treatment was necessary to achieve the compelling state interest. The court concluded that the designation of "marriage" would not have an impact on opposite-sex couples. However, the court concluded that a separate and differently named family for same-sex couples would be harmful to the couples as well as their offspring due to a possible perception that such a union is of a "lesser stature" in comparison to relationships of opposite-sex couples. The court concluded that the state's domestic partnership law provides insufficient protections to same-sex couples. Specifically, the court stated that "[r]etaining the designation of marriage exclusively for opposite-sex couples and providing only a separate and distinct designation for same-sex couples may well have the effect of perpetuating a more general premise—now emphatically rejected by this state—that gay individuals and same-sex couples are in some respects 'second-class citizens.'" As such, the court found such a distinction unconstitutional under the California constitution.

Presumably in reaction to the California Supreme Court's holding, on November 4, 2008, California voters approved a constitutional amendment (Proposition 8) limiting the validity and recognition of "marriages" to heterosexual couples. This constitutional amendment appears to be intended to overrule the California Supreme Court's decision. However, legal challenges were filed seeking injunctive relief against the amendment's implementation. On November 19, 2008, the court denied the requests for injunctive relief. However, the court agreed to decide three

---

[108] *Id.*

[109] *Id.* at 433.

[110] Under the federal law, classification or discrimination based on gender is subject to intermediate scrutiny as opposed to strict scrutiny. However, California courts have employed strict scrutiny analysis, thus guaranteeing greater protection against gender discrimination. For example, in *Woods v. Horton*, the court employed a strict scrutiny analysis in finding unconstitutional a state statute that funded certain domestic violence programs only for female victims and their children. 84 Cal.Rptr. 3d 332 (Cal. App. 3 Dist. October 14, 2008).

[111] *See,* 183 P.3d 384, 444 (rejecting the argument that a group's current political powerlessness is a prerequisite in the classification of "suspect" class by stating that "it would be impossible to justify the numerous decisions that continue to treat sex, race, and religion as suspect classifications.").

issues regarding Proposition 8's validity and/or retroactivity, including (1) whether Proposition 8 was a constitutional amendment or revision, (2) the validity of the initiative process itself, and (3) whether Proposition 8 itself is retroactive, applying to existing same-sex marriages.[112]

On May 26, 2009, the California Supreme Court concluded that Proposition 8 is a properly enacted limited constitutional amendment, not a constitutional revision requiring a two-thirds vote of the legislature to be placed before voters.[113] The court noted that precedent establishes the criteria for determining whether a constitutional change constitutes a revision rather than an amendment. A court must assess "(1) the meaning and scope of the constitutional change at issue, and (2) the effect—both quantitative and qualitative—that the constitutional change will have on the basic governmental plan or framework embodied in the preexisting provisions of the California Constitution."[114] Concluding that Proposition 8 is a constitutional amendment, the court analyzed its quantitative and qualitative effect on the preexisting provisions of the state constitution and reasoned that the amendment does not repeal or abrogate same-sex couples' constitutional rights of privacy and due process or fundamentally alter "the meaning and substance" of equal protection principles recognized in the court's previous ruling pertaining to same-sex marriage and in laws allowing civil unions. Instead, the court stated that

> [t]he measure carves out a narrow and limited exception to the state constitutional rights, reserving the official designation of the term "marriage" for the union of opposite-sex couples as a matter of state constitutional law, but leaving undisturbed all of the other extremely significant aspects of a same-sex couple's state constitutional right to establish an officially recognized and protected family relationship and the guarantee of equal protection of the laws.[115]

Unlike its previous decision, the court did not explicitly address whether a parallel structure, such as a civil union, would maintain same-sex couples' constitutional privacy, due process, and equal protection rights. However, it might be inferred from the court's characterization of Proposition 8[116] that it now believes that a parallel structure would comport with constitutional requirements.

In addressing the status of same-sex marriages performed before Proposition 8's passage, the court unanimously found that the amendment applies prospectively. The court noted that ending such marriages would be akin to "throwing property rights into disarray, destroying the legal interests and expectations of thousands of couples and their families, and potentially undermining the ability of citizens to plan their lives according to the law as it has been determined by the state's highest court."[117] As such, the court held that such marriages remain valid and must continue to be recognized within the state.[118]

---

[112] *Strauss v. Horton*, No. S168047/S168066/S168078 (Ca. November 19, 2008).

[113] *Strauss v. Horton*, 207 P.3d 48 (Ca. 2009). Under the California constitution, the initiative process may be used to propose and adopt constitutional amendments but may not be used to revise the state constitution.

[114] *Id.* at 61.

[115] *Id.*

[116] As noted earlier in this report, the court concluded that Proposition 8 as a constitutional amendment merely defined the term "marriage" as officially used within the state and, therefore, did not fundamentally alter "a same-sex couple's ... right to establish an officially recognized and protected family relationship." *Id.*

[117] *Id.* at 121.

[118] In the aftermath of *Strauss*, at least one complaint has been filed in district court seeking declaratory and injunctive relief alleging that Proposition 8 is unconstitutional under the Due Process and Equal Protection Clauses of the 14th Amendment of the U.S. Constitution.

On August 4, 2010, a U.S. district court for the Northern District of California found that Proposition 8 was unconstitutional under the Fourteenth Amendment to the U.S. Constitution's Due Process and Equal Protection Clauses.[119] In deciding the Due Process question, the court considered two issues: (1) what type of right did the plaintiffs seek to exercise and (2) the appropriate standard of review. The threshold issue was whether the plaintiffs sought to exercise the fundamental right to marry or if they were seeking recognition of a new right. After considering the evidence presented at trial, the court concluded that the plaintiffs sought the former. Following a similar analysis to the California Supreme Court, the district court concluded that marriage has retained certain characteristics throughout history including the requirement that two parties give their free consent to form a relationship, which then forms the foundation of a household.[120] The court found that the evidence shows that there has been a "movement of marriage away from a gendered institution and toward an institution free from state-mandated gender roles."

The district court concluded that as the plaintiffs sought to exercise their fundamental right to marry, the appropriate standard for analysis would be strict scrutiny. However, instead of applying this analysis, the court found that Proposition 8 could not withstand a substantially lower standard of "rational basis" review citing similar factors articulated by previous state courts. As to the strict scrutiny analysis, the court stated that "the minimal evidentiary presentation made by proponents does not meet the heavy burden of production necessary to show that Proposition 8 is narrowly tailored to a compelling government interest. Proposition 8 cannot, therefore, withstand strict scrutiny."[121]

In addressing the equal protection claim, the court declined to address whether laws classifying on the basis of sexual orientation should be subject to a heightened standard of review despite opining that such should be required. Instead, the court found that Proposition 8 does not survive rational basis, citing the same reasons as previous state courts.[122] Additionally, the court noted:

> An initiative measure adopted by the voters deserves great respect.... When challenged, however, the voters' determinations must find at least some support in evidence. This is especially so when those determinations enact into law classifications of persons. Conjecture, speculation and fears are not enough. Still less will the moral disapprobation of a group or class of citizens suffice, no matter how large the majority that shares that view. The evidence demonstrated beyond serious reckoning that Proposition 8 finds support only in such disapproval.[123]

The court's determination that denying the right to same-sex marriage warrants a heightened level of review may affect other laws related to discrimination based on sexual orientation. While the decision is currently limited, the rationale may be applied in other state challenges. On February 7, 2012, a panel of the Ninth Circuit Court of Appeals affirmed the district court's decision, albeit on much narrower grounds.[124] In reaching its decision, the appellate court relied on the U.S.

---

[119] *Perry v. Schwarzenegger*, 704 F.Supp.2d 921 (N.D. Ca. August 4, 2010).

[120] *Id.* at 992.

[121] *Id.* at 994.

[122] *Id.* at 938.

[123] *Id.* at 938.

[124] 2012 WL 372712, *12 (C.A.9 (Cal.)) (stating that "... this argument applies to the specific history of California, it is the narrowest ground for adjudicating the constitutional questions before us.").

Supreme Court's decision in *Romer v. Evans*[125] where the Court struck down a Colorado initiative that prevented local governments from passing anti-discrimination ordinances to protect gays and lesbians. As discussed above, the *Romer* Court held that the federal Constitution prevents states from taking away rights based on moral disapproval. The Ninth Circuit court found similarities between the Colorado and California initiatives, inasmuch as both "single[d] out a certain class of citizens for disfavored legal status...."[126] While the court acknowledged Proposition 8 was more limited than the Colorado initiative, it still found *Romer* applicable. Just as in *Romer*, the court concluded that there was no legitimate state interest to constitute a rational basis for Proposition 8.[127] As such, the court inferred that "Proposition 8 was born out of disapproval of gays and lesbians"[128] and violates the Equal Protection Clause.[129]

The intervenors have the option of seeking review by the full circuit panel or appealing directly to the U.S. Supreme Court. It is unclear whether the Court would accept the case for review on the merits as it pertains to an interpretation of a state constitutional amendment. Moreover, in the absence of a circuit split, the Court may decline to review the matter.

The Connecticut and Iowa supreme courts agreed with the California Supreme Court's finding that laws discriminating against homosexuals must be subjected to a higher level of scrutiny. However, these courts declined to use a strict scrutiny analysis. Instead, the courts used a variety of factors to determine that sexual orientation is a quasi-suspect class analogous to gender, thus warranting an intermediate scrutiny analysis.[130] In exploring the nature of homosexual identity, the history of societal views regarding homosexuality, and the limitation of political power possessed by homosexuals, the courts found that homosexuals suffered a history of invidious discrimination based on characteristics not within their control that bear "no relation to [their] ability to perform or contribute to society."[131] Therefore, the courts concluded that homosexuals are a quasi-suspect class requiring the state to advance a sufficiently persuasive justification for denying same-sex couples the right to marry. As in the Massachusetts and California decisions, the Connecticut and Iowa supreme courts rejected the state's justifications of promoting uniformity and preserving the traditional definition of marriage.[132]

New Jersey

Similarly, on October 25, 2006, the New Jersey Supreme Court held that the state's constitution requires that same-sex couples be granted the same legal rights as married heterosexual couples. However, the court declined to label those rights and instead ordered the state legislature to

---

[125] 517 U.S. 620 (1996).

[126] *Perry v. Brown*, Nos. 10-16696, 11-16577, 2012 WL 372713, at *1, *16 (C.A. 9 (Cal., February 7, 2012)). One of the issues before the court was whether the intervenors had standing to appeal the lower court's decision. The Ninth Circuit found that the parties did have the requisite standing. *Id.* at *7.

[127] *Id.* at *17.

[128] *Id.* at *27.

[129] *Id.* at *28.

[130] It was also a matter of first impression for the Connecticut court to classify sexual orientation as a quasi-suspect class.

[131] *Kerrigan v. Commissioner of Public Health*, 957 A.2d 407, 425 (Conn. 2008).

[132] *Id.* at 473; *Varnum v. Brien*, 763 N.W.2d 862 (Iowa 2009).

amend its marriage statutes or enact a new statutory scheme granting the state's same-sex couples the rights of married couples within 180 days.[133]

In its 4-3 decision,[134] the majority separated the plaintiffs' equal protection argument into two questions: (1) whether committed same-sex couples have a constitutional right to the benefits and privileges afforded to married heterosexual couples and (2) if so, whether they have the constitutional right to have their permanent committed relationship recognized by the name "marriage."[135] In addressing the first question, the court discussed New Jersey's recent history of passing laws providing benefits to same-sex couples. For example, the state forbids sexual orientation discrimination and allows same-sex couples to become foster parents as well as adopt children. The court concluded that the state's statutes and judicial opinions provide committed same-sex couples with a strong interest in equality of treatment.[136] Moreover, the court concluded that although the state's Domestic Partnership Act provided same-sex couples with some important rights, the act failed to "bridge the inequality gap between committed same-sex couples and married opposite-sex couples."[137]

The court held that the state has no legitimate interest in denying the benefits and privileges of marriage to same-sex couples.[138] In assessing the public need for denying committed same-sex couples the full benefits and privileges that flow from marriage, the court rejected the state's argument of uniformity with other states and concluded that the disparate treatment of committed same-sex couples directly disadvantages their children. Moreover, the court concluded that there "is no rational basis for, on the one hand, giving gays and lesbians full civil rights in their status as individuals, and, on the other, giving them an incomplete set of rights when they follow the inclination of their sexual orientation and enter into committed same-sex relationships."[139] As such, the court found that denying committed same-sex couples the financial and social benefits and privileges given to married heterosexual couples bears no substantial relationship to a legitimate government purpose.

However, the court held that there is no fundamental due process right to same-sex marriage encompassed within the concept of "liberty" guaranteed by the state constitution. In reaching its decision, the court adopted the general standard followed by the U.S. Supreme Court in construing the Due Process Clause of the Fourteenth Amendment of the U.S. Constitution. The court found that there was no legal or historical basis for same-sex marriage nor anything to suggest that the framers of the federal or state constitutions considered it a fundamental right to be afforded special protection. The court emphasized the importance of tradition to substantive due process analysis—and held that, according to tradition, the right to marry a same-sex partner

---

[133] *Lewis v. Harris*, 908 A.2d 196 (NJ 2006) (stating that "the name to be given to the statutory scheme that provides full rights and benefits to same-sex couples, whether marriage or some other term, is a matter left to the democratic process."). As this decision is based solely on New Jersey's state constitution, it is not reviewable by the U.S. Supreme Court.

[134] This was an unanimous decision as to providing benefits and protections to same-sex couples. The dissent concurred in granting benefits and protections but dissented in that they believed that the name "marriage" was also required. *Id.*

[135] *Id.* at 212.

[136] *Id.* at 215.

[137] *Id.*

[138] *Id.* at 218 (stating that "in light of the policies reflected in the statutory and decisional laws of the state, we cannot find a legitimate public need for an unequal legal scheme of benefits and privileges that disadvantages committed same-sex couples.").

[139] *Id.* at 217.

is not "deeply rooted in our nation's history."[140] As a result, the court declined to find a fundamental right to same-sex marriage. Instead, the court ordered the legislature to provide to committed same-sex couples the "full rights and benefits enjoyed by heterosexual couples."[141] The court provided two options to the legislature: (1) amend the marriage statutes to include same-sex couples; or (2) enact a parallel statutory structure by another name, in which same-sex couples would receive the same rights and benefits as well as the "burdens and obligations of civil marriage."[142]

Arizona

Although the aforementioned opinions deal primarily with a state constitution,[143] an Arizona Court of Appeals, exercising its discretion to accept jurisdiction based on the issue of first impression, held that the fundamental right to marry protected by the Fourteenth Amendment of the U.S. Constitution as well as the Arizona Constitution did not encompass the right to marry a same-sex partner.[144] Moreover, the court found that the state had a legitimate interest in encouraging procreation and child rearing within the marital relationship and limiting that relationship to opposite-sex couples.

In light of the Supreme Court's decision in *Lawrence*, the petitioners argued that the Arizona statute prohibiting same-sex marriages violated their fundamental right to marry and their right to equal protection under the laws, both of which are guaranteed by the federal and state constitutions. The Arizona court rejected the petitioners' argument that the Supreme Court in *Lawrence* implicitly recognized that the fundamental right to marry includes the freedom to choose a same-sex spouse.[145] The court viewed the *Lawrence* language as acknowledging a homosexual person's "right to define his or her own existence, and achieve the type of individual fulfillment that is the hallmark of a free society, by entering a homosexual relationship."[146] However, the court declined to view the language as stating that such a right includes the choice to enter a state-sanctioned, same-sex marriage.[147]

As such, the court reviewed the constitutionality of the challenged statutes using a rational basis analysis and found that the state has a legitimate interest in encouraging procreation and child-

---

[140] *Id.* at 206.

[141] *Id.* at 223.

[142] *Id.* The New Jersey legislature passed a civil union bill on December 15, 2006, which became effective February 2007.

[143] The Maryland Supreme Court ruled that limiting marriage to a man and a woman does not discriminate against gay couples or deny them constitutional rights. In addition, the court stated that the state's prohibition on same-sex marriage promotes the state's interest in heterosexual marriage as a means of having and protecting children. *Conaway v. Deane*, 932 A.2d 571 (MD 2007). Similar results have occurred in New York and Washington. See, *Hernandez v. Robles*, 855 N.E.2d 1 (N.Y. 2006); *Anderson v. King County*, 138 P.3d 963 (Wash. 2006). There are approximately 20 lawsuits filed that seek same-sex marriage rights under state constitutions. These states include Florida, Indiana, Nebraska, and Oregon.

[144] *Standhardt v. Superior Court of the State of Arizona*, 77 P.3d 451 (Ariz. Ct. App. 2003).

[145] *Id.* at 457.

[146] *Id.*

[147] See also, *Morrison v. Sadler*, 2003 WL 23119998 (Ind. Super. May 7, 2003)(holding that the state's law "promotes the state's interest in encouraging procreation to occur in a context where both biological parents are present to raise the child."); *Lewis v. Harris*, 2003 WL 23191114 (N.J.Super.L. November 5, 2003)(holding that the right to marry does not include a fundamental right to same-sex marriage).

---

rearing within the marital relationship, and that limiting marriage to opposite-sex couples is rationally related to that interest. Moreover, the court said that while the state's reasoning is debatable, it is not arbitrary or irrational. Consequently, the court upheld the challenged statutes.

State "Civil Union" Laws

Civil union/domestic partnership laws confer certain rights and benefits upon domestic partners, which vary depending on state law. Some of these rights and benefits include laws relating to title, tenure, descent and distribution, intestate succession; causes of action related to or dependent upon spousal status,[148] including an action for wrongful death,[149] emotional distress, or loss of consortium; probate law and procedure; adoption law and procedure; insurance benefits; workers' compensation rights; laws relating to medical care and treatment, hospital visitation and notification; family leave benefits; and public assistance benefits under state laws and laws relating to state taxes.[150]

For example, in Vermont, civil union status[151] is available to two persons of the same sex who are unrelated[152] and affords parties "the same benefits, protections and responsibilities under Vermont law, whether they derive from statute, policy, administrative or court rule, common law or any other source of civil law, as are granted to spouses in a marriage."[153] Civil union status is also available in Connecticut,[154] Hawaii,[155] New Hampshire,[156] and New Jersey.[157] Domestic partnership laws in California,[158] Hawaii,[159] New Jersey,[160] Oregon,[161] and Washington[162] also

---

[148] See *Salucco v. Alldredge*, 17 Mass. L. Rptr. 498 (Mass. Super., 2004)(exercising its general equity jurisdiction to dissolve a Vermont civil union).

[149] See *Langan v. St. Vincent Hosp.*, 196 Misc.2d 440 (N.Y. Misc. 2003)(finding that New York's statutes did not prohibit recognition of a same-sex union nor was such a union against New York's public policy on marriage thus recognizing the same-sex partner as a spouse for purposes of New York's wrongful death statute), overruled by *Langan v. St. Vincent Hosp.*, 802 N.Y.S. 2d 476 (NY AD 2 Dept., 2005).

[150] Constitutional amendments approved in Arkansas, Georgia, Kansas, Kentucky, Michigan, North Dakota, Oklahoma, Ohio and Utah contain language which state that a legal status which is substantially similar to marriage (i.e., civil unions or domestic partnerships) may not be recognized.

[151] On April 7, 2009, Vermont state legislators overrode the governor's veto of a bill legalizing same-sex marriage. It is unclear as to whether civil unions will remain available to same-sex couples.

[152] Vt. Stat. Ann. Tit. 15 §§1203, 5163. See also, "The Vermont Guide to Civil Unions," found at http://www.sec.state.vt.us/otherprg/civilunions/civilunions html.

[153] Vt. Stat. Ann. Tit. 15 §1204. See also, *Salucco v. Alldredge*, 17 Mass. L. Rptr. 498 (Mass. Super., 2004)(discussing Vermont's civil union statutes).

[154] Connecticut's civil union laws became effective October 1, 2005. A Connecticut civil union is available to an individual at least 18 years of age, of the same sex as the other party to the civil union, no more closely related to the other than first cousin and not a party to another civil union or marriage. 2005 Conn. Legis. Serv. P.A. 05-10 (S.S.B. 963).

[155] Effective January 1, 2012.

[156] New Hampshire's civil union laws became effective January 1, 2008. A New Hampshire civil union is available to an individual at least 18 years of age, of the same sex as the other party to the civil union, no more closely related to the other than first cousin and not a party to another civil union or marriage. N.H. Rev. Stat. §§457-A:2-4.

[157] New Jersey's civil union laws became effective February 2007.

[158] CA Fam. §§297, 298 and 299(extending the rights and duties of marriage to persons registered as domestic partners on and after January 1, 2005). It should be noted that opposite-sex domestic partners over the age of 62 meeting the eligibility requirements of Title II of the Social Security Act (SSA) for old age benefits (as defined in 42 U.S.C. §402(a)), or Title XVI of the SSA for aged individuals (as defined in 42 U.S.C. §1381) are eligible to register as domestic partners.

---

offer some marital benefits to same-sex couples, although not as comprehensive as Vermont's or Connecticut's civil unions.[163]

Congressional Activity

In recent years, several bills have been introduced to address the issue of same-sex marriage. For example, in the 112th Congress, H.R. 875 (the Marriage Protection Act) was introduced, and would amend Title 28 of the *United States Code* to limit federal court jurisdiction over legal questions regarding DOMA.[164] Also introduced in the 112th Congress, H.R. 1116/S. 598 (the Respect for Marriage Act) would repeal the definitions of "marriage" and "spouse" found in Section 3 of DOMA (28 U.S.C. §1738C). Instead, these bills would impose no specific federal definition of these terms, but would consider parties married for purposes of federal law if certain conditions are met. These conditions are (1) that the marriage, if entered into in a state,[165] must be valid in that state and (2) if the marriage was not entered into in a state,[166] that it could have been entered into in a state.

There have also been bills introduced in previous Congresses addressing federal recognition of same-sex marriages.[167] For example, in the 110th Congress, H.J.Res. 22, a proposed amendment to the U.S. Constitution, was introduced. The text of the proposed amendment was as follows:

> Section 1. Marriage in the United States shall consist only of a legal union of one man and one woman.

(...continued)

[159] Hawaii's term for domestic partners is "reciprocal beneficiaries." Reciprocal beneficiaries must be eighteen years old, ineligible to marry, and unmarried. This status includes relationships not involving sex or the same residence. Haw. Rev. Stat. §572C-5; See also, http://www.hawaii.gov/health/vital-records/vital-records/reciprocal/index.html (discussing Hawaii's reciprocal beneficiary status).

[160] The New Jersey Domestic Partnership Act became effective July 11, 2004, and grants legal status to same-sex couples and unmarried, opposite-sex couples age 62 or over under certain New Jersey laws.

[161] Oregon's domestic partnership laws went into effect on January 1, 2008.

[162] Washington's domestic partnership laws went into effect on July 22, 2007.

[163] Domestic partnerships also exist at the local level. For example, New York City allows residents an opportunity to register their domestic partnerships provided that both individuals are eighteen years of age or older, unmarried or related by blood in a manner that would bar his or her marriage in New York State, have a close and committed personal relationship, live together and have been living together on a continuous basis. N.Y.C. Admin. Code §3-241. It should be noted that this statute allows both same-sex and opposite-sex partners to register.

[164] H.R. 875 is identical to H.R. 3313, the Marriage Protection Act of 2004, introduced during the 108th Congress. On July 22, 2004, the House voted on and passed H.R. 3313. The Senate did not consider the legislation during the 108th Congress. Similar bills were introduced in the 109th (H.R. 1100) and 110th (H.R. 724) Congresses.

[165] The bill's definition of state encompasses the 50 states, the District of Columbia, Puerto Rico and "any other territory or possession of the United States."

[166] For example, Canada or the Netherlands.

[167] H.J.Res. 22 was introduced in the 110th Congress. S.J.Res. 1, S.J.Res. 13, H.J.Res. 39, and H.J.Res. 91 were introduced in the 109th Congress. On June 7, 2006, the Senate considered and voted on a required procedural motion regarding S.J.Res. 1. This motion failed by a vote of 49-48, which prevented further consideration of S.J.Res. 1. In addition, H.J.Res. 56, S.J.Res. 26, S.J.Res. 30, S.J.Res. 40, and H.J.Res. 106 were introduced in the 108th Congress. On July 14, 2004, the Senate considered and voted on a required procedural motion. This motion failed by a vote of 48-50, which prevented further consideration of S.J.Res. 40. On September 30, 2004, the House failed to pass H.J.Res. 106 by a vote of 227-186.

Section 2. No court of the United States or of any State shall have jurisdiction to determine whether this Constitution or the constitution of any State requires that the legal incidents of marriage be conferred upon any union other than a legal union between one man and one woman.

Section 3. No State shall be required to give effect to any public act, record, or judicial proceeding of any other State concerning a union between persons of the same sex that is treated as a marriage, or as having the legal incidents of marriage, under the laws of such other State.

Also introduced in the 110th Congress, H.R. 107 would have defined marriage for all legal purposes in the District of Columbia to consist of the union of one man and one woman.[168]

Although national uniformity may be achieved upon ratification of one of the proposed amendments to the U.S. Constitution,[169] states would no longer have the flexibility of defining marriage within their borders. Moreover, states may be prohibited from recognizing a same-sex marriage performed and recognized outside of the United States.[170] Some of the proposed amendments may affect a state's ability to define civil unions or domestic partnerships and the benefits conferred upon such.

A further complication in the definition of marriage may arise regarding the determination of an individual's gender. As the first official document to indicate a person's sex, the designation on the birth certificate "usually controls the sex designation on all later documents."[171] Some courts have held that sexual identity for purposes of marriage is determined by the sex stated on the birth certificate, regardless of subsequent sexual reassignment.[172] However, some argue that this method is flawed, as an infant's sex may be misidentified at birth and the individual may subsequently identify with and conform his or her biology to another sex upon adulthood.[173]

Conclusion

States currently possess the authority to decide whether to recognize an out-of-state marriage. The Full Faith and Credit Clause has rarely been used by states to validate marriages because marriages are not "legal judgments." With respect to cases decided under the Full Faith and Credit Clause that involve conflicting state statutes, the Supreme Court generally examines the significant aggregation of contacts the forum has with the parties and the occurrence or transaction to decide which state's law to apply. Similarly, based upon generally accepted legal

---

[168] H.R. 107 was introduced on January 4, 2007.

[169] The proposed constitutional amendment would have to be ratified by three-quarters of the states (either the legislatures thereof, or in amendment conventions).

[170] It appears that the Netherlands, Belgium, Canada, South Africa, Norway, and Spain are the only international jurisdictions that sanction and/or recognize a same-sex union as a "marriage," per se.

[171] Julie A. Greenberg, Defining Male and Female: Intersexuality and the Collision Between Law and Biology, 41 Ariz. L. Rev. 265,309 (1999) (discussing biological characteristics and sexual identity).

[172] *See, e.g., In re Estate of Gardiner*, 42 P.3d 120 (Kan. 2002); *Littleton v. Prange*, 9 S.W. 3d 223 (Tex. App. 1999); but see, *M.T. v. J.T.*, 355 A.2d 204 (N.J. 1976)(determining an individual's sexual classification for the purpose of marriage encompasses a mental component as well as an anatomical component).

[173] If a mistake was made on the original birth certificate, an amended certificate will sometimes be issued if accompanied by an affidavit from a physician or a court order.

---

principles, states routinely decide whether a marriage validly contracted in another jurisdiction will be recognized in-state by examining whether it has a significant relationship with the spouses and the marriage. Congress is empowered under the Full Faith and Credit Clause of the Constitution to prescribe the manner that public acts, commonly understood to mean legislative acts, records, and proceedings shall be proved and the effect of such acts, records, and proceedings in other states.[174]

The Supreme Court's decisions in *Romer v. Colorado* and *Lawrence v. Texas* may present different issues concerning DOMA's constitutionality. Basically *Romer* appears to stand for the proposition that legislation targeting gays and lesbians is constitutionally impermissible under the Equal Protection Clause unless the legislative classification bears a rational relationship to a legitimate state purpose. Because same-sex marriages are singled out for differential treatment, DOMA appears to create a legislative classification for equal protection purposes that must meet a rational basis test. It is possible that DOMA would survive constitutional scrutiny under *Romer*, inasmuch as the statute was enacted to protect the traditional institution of marriage. Moreover, DOMA does not prohibit states from recognizing same-sex marriage if they so choose.

Lawrence appears to stand for the proposition that the zone of privacy protected by the Due Process Clause of the Fourteen Amendment extends to adult, consensual sex between homosexuals. *Lawrence's* implication for statutes banning same-sex marriages and the constitutional validity of the DOMA are unclear.

Lower courts have begun to address DOMA's constitutionality. Historically, the federal government has deferred to a state's definition of marriage. However, with the legalization of same-sex marriage in several jurisdictions, federal agencies continue to grapple with the interplay of DOMA and the distribution of federal marriage-based benefits. Lower courts have found DOMA to violate equal protection principles, state sovereignty, and Congress's authority under its spending power. It would appear that there is a possibility that district and/or circuit courts will disagree on DOMA's constitutionality. Such a split could cause changes in the distribution of federal marriage-based benefits depending on a same-sex couple's residence, thus making it more likely that one of these cases will reach the U.S. Supreme Court.

State Constitutional Amendments Limiting Marriage to a Man and a Woman

Alabama

> Marriage is inherently a unique relationship between a man and a woman. As a matter of public policy, this state has a special interest in encouraging, supporting, and protecting this unique relationship in order to promote, among other goals, the stability and welfare of

---

[174] It should be noted that only on five occasions previous to the DOMA has Congress enacted legislation based upon this power. The first, passed in 1790 (1 Stat. 122, codified at 28 U.S.C. §1738), provides for ways to authenticate acts, records and judicial proceedings. The second, dating from 1804 (2 Stat. 298, codified at 28 U.S.C. 1738), provides methods of authenticating non-judicial records. Three other congressional enactments pertain to modifiable family law orders (child custody, 28 U.S.C. §1738A; child support, 28 U.S.C. §1738B; and domestic protection, 18 U.S.C. §2265).

society and its children. A marriage contracted between individuals of the same sex is invalid in this state.

Marriage is a sacred covenant, solemnized between a man and a woman, which, when the legal capacity and consent of both parties is present, establishes their relationship as husband and wife, and which is recognized by the state as a civil contract.

No marriage license shall be issued in the state of Alabama to parties of the same sex.

The state of Alabama shall not recognize as valid any marriage of parties of the same sex that occurred or was alleged to have occurred as a result of the law of any jurisdiction regardless of whether a marriage license was issued.

The state of Alabama shall not recognize as valid any common law marriage of parties of the same sex.

A union replicating marriage of or between persons of the same sex in the state of Alabama or in any other jurisdiction shall be considered and treated in all respects as having no legal force or effect in this state and shall not be recognized by this state as a marriage or other union replicating marriage.[175]

Arkansas

Marriage consists only of the union of one man and one woman. Legal status for unmarried persons which is identical or substantially similar to marital status shall not be valid or recognized in Arkansas, except that the Legislature may recognize a common law marriage from another state between a man and a woman. The Legislature has the power to determine the capacity of persons to marry, subject to this amendment, and the legal rights, obligations, privileges and immunities of marriage.[176]

Arizona

Only a union of one man and one woman shall be valid or recognized as marriage in this state.[177]

California

Only marriage between a man and a woman is valid and recognized in California.[178]

Colorado

Only a union of one man and one woman shall be valid or recognized as a marriage in this state.[179]

---

[175] 2005 Ala. Acts 35.

[176] AR. CONST. Amend. 83, §1.

[177] A.Z. CONST. Art. 30.

[178] CA CONST. Art. 1, §7.5.

[179] CO. CONST. Art. II, §31.

Florida

Inasmuch as marriage is the legal union of only one man and one woman as husband and wife, no other legal union that is treated as marriage or the substantial equivalent thereof shall be valid or recognized.[180]

Georgia

This state shall recognize as marriage only the union of man and woman. Marriages between persons of the same sex are prohibited in this state. No union between persons of the same sex shall be recognized by this state as entitled to the benefits of marriage. This state shall not give effect to any public act, record or judicial proceeding of any other state or jurisdiction respecting a relationship between persons of the same sex that is treated as a marriage under the laws of such other state or jurisdiction. The courts of this state shall have no jurisdiction to grant a divorce or separate maintenance with respect to any such relationship or otherwise to consider or rule on any of the parties' respective rights arising as a result of or in connection with such relationship.[181]

Idaho

A marriage between a man and a woman is the only domestic legal union that shall be valid or recognized in this state.[182]

Kansas

The marriage contract is to be considered in law as a civil contract. Marriage shall be constituted by one man and one woman only. All other marriages are declared to be contrary to the public policy of this state and are void.

No relationship, other than a marriage, shall be recognized by the state as entitling the parties to the rights or incidents of marriage.[183]

Kentucky

Only a marriage between one man and one woman shall be valid or recognized as a marriage in Kentucky. A legal status identical or substantially similar to that of marriage for unmarried individuals shall not be valid or recognized.[184]

---

[180] FLA CONST. Art. I.

[181] GA. CONST. Art. I., §IV. On May 16, 2006, a state county court stuck down Georgia's constitutional amendment on the grounds that it violated a rule that limits ballot questions to a single subject. *O'Kelley, et. al v. Perdue*, 2004CV93494 (Super. Ct. Fulton County, GA May 16, 2006).

[182] ID CONST. Art. III, §28.

[183] KS CONST. Art. 15, §16.

[184] KY. CONST. §233A.

Louisiana

Marriage in the state of Louisiana shall consist only of the union of one man and one woman. No official or court of the state of Louisiana shall construe this constitution or any state law to require that marriage or the legal incidents thereof be conferred upon any member of a union other than the union of one man and one woman. A legal status identical or substantially similar to that of marriage for unmarried individuals shall not be valid or recognized. No official or court of the state of Louisiana shall recognize any marriage contracted in any other jurisdiction which is not the union of one man and one woman to the state constitution.[185]

Michigan

To secure and preserve the benefits of marriage for our society and for future generations of children, the union of one man and one woman in marriage shall be the only agreement recognized as a marriage or similar union for any purpose.[186]

Mississippi

Marriage may take place and may be valid under the laws of this state only between a man and a woman. A marriage in another state or foreign jurisdiction between persons of the same gender, regardless of when the marriage took place, may not be recognized in this state and is void and unenforceable under the laws of this state.[187]

Missouri

That to be valid and recognized in this state, a marriage shall exist only between a man and a woman.[188]

Montana

Only a marriage between one man and one woman shall be valid or recognized as a marriage in this state.

North Carolina

Marriage between one man and one woman is the only domestic legal union that shall be valid or recognized in this State. This section does not prohibit a private party from entering

---

[185] LA. CONST. Art. XII, §15. The Louisiana Supreme Court reversed a state district judge's ruling striking down the amendment on the grounds that it violated a provision of the state constitution requiring that an amendment cover only one subject. The Court found that each provision of the amendment is germane to the single object of defense of marriage and constitutes an element of the plan advanced to achieve this object. *Forum for Equality PAC v. McKeithen,* 893 So. 2d 715 (La., 2005).

[186] MI. CONST., Art. 1, §25.

[187] MISS. CONST. §263-A.

[188] MO. CONST., Art. I, Sect. 33.

---

into contracts with another private party; nor does this section prohibit courts from adjudicating the rights of private parties pursuant to such contracts.[189]

North Dakota

Marriage consists only of the legal union between a man and a woman. No other domestic union, however denominated, may be recognized as a marriage or given the same or substantially equivalent effect.

Ohio

Only a union between one man and one woman may be a marriage valid in or recognized by this state and its political subdivisions. This state and its political subdivisions shall not create or recognize a legal status for relationships of unmarried individuals that intends to approximate the design, qualities, significance or effect of marriage.

Oklahoma

Marriage in this state shall consist only of the union of one man and one woman. Neither this constitution nor any other provision of law shall be construed to require that marital status or the legal incidents thereof be conferred upon unmarried couples or groups. A marriage between persons of the same gender performed in another state shall not be recognized as valid and binding in this state as of the date of the marriage. Any person knowingly issuing a marriage license in violation of this section shall be guilty of a misdemeanor.[190]

Oregon

It is the policy of Oregon, and its political subdivisions, that only a marriage between one man and one woman shall be valid or legally recognized as a marriage.[191]

South Carolina

Marriage in the state of South Carolina, and its political subdivisions, is exclusively defined as a union between one man and one woman; all other attempted or putative unions, including those recognized by other jurisdictions are void ab initio.[192]

South Dakota

Only marriage between a man and a woman shall be valid or recognized in South Dakota. The uniting of two or more persons in a civil union, domestic partnership, or other quasi-marital relationship shall not be valid or recognized in South Dakota.[193]

---

[189] NC CONST. Art. XIV, §6.

[190] OKLA. CONST. Art. II, §35.

[191] OR. CONST. Art. XV, §5a.

[192] SC CONST. Art. XVII, §15.

[193] SD CONST. Art. XXI, §9.

Tennessee

The historical institution and legal contract solemnizing the relationship of one man and one woman shall be the only legally recognized marital contract in this state. Any policy or law or judicial interpretation, purporting to define marriage as anything other than the historical institution and legal contract between one man and one woman, is contrary to the public policy of this state and shall be void and unenforceable in Tennessee. If another state or foreign jurisdiction issues a license for persons to marry and if such marriage is prohibited in this state by the provisions of this section, then the marriage shall be void and unenforceable in this state.[194]

Texas

Marriage in this state shall consist only of the union of one man and one woman. This state or a political subdivision of this state may not create or recognize any legal status identical or similar to marriage.[195]

Utah

Marriage consists only of the legal union between a man and a woman. No other domestic status or union, however denominated, between persons is valid or recognized or may be authorized, sanctioned or given the same or substantially equivalent legal effect as a marriage.[196]

Virginia

Only a union between one man and one woman may be a marriage valid in or recognized by this Commonwealth and its political subdivisions. This Commonwealth and its political subdivisions shall not create or recognize a legal status for relationships of unmarried individuals that intends to approximate the design, qualities, significance, or effects of marriage. Nor shall this Commonwealth or its political subdivisions create or recognize another union, partnership, or other legal status to which is assigned the rights, benefits, obligations, qualities, or effects of marriage.[197]

Wisconsin

Only a marriage between one man and one woman shall be valid or recognized as a marriage in this state. A legal status identical or substantially similar to that of marriage for unmarried individuals shall not be valid or recognized in this state.[198]

---

[194] TN CONST. Art. XI, §3.

[195] TX CONST. Art. 1, §32.

[196] UTAH CONST. Art. I, §29.

[197] VA CONST. Art. I, §15-A.

[198] WI CONST. Art. XIII, §3.

Table 1. State Statutes Defining "Marriage"

State	Statute	Marriage Definition[a]	Non-Recognition
Alabama	Ala. Code §30-1-19 (2011)	X	X
Alaska	Alaska Stat. §25.05.011 (2011)	X	
Arizona	Ariz. Rev. Stat. §25-101 (2011)		X
Arkansas	Ark. Code Ann. §9-11-109 (2011)	X	
California	Judicial Interpretation	X[b]	
Colorado	Colo. Rev. Stat. §14-2-104 (2011)	X	
Connecticut	Judicial Interpretation		X[c]
Delaware	Del. Code Ann. tit. 13, §101 (2011)		X
Florida	Fla. Stat. Ann. §741.04 (2012)	X	
Georgia	Ga. Code Ann. §19-3-3.1 (2011)		X
Hawaii	Haw. Rev. Stat. Ann. §572-1 (2011)	X	
Idaho*	Idaho Code Ann. §32-209 (2011)	X	
Illinois*	750 Ill. Comp. Stat. Ann. 5/201 (2012)	X	X
Indiana	Ind. Code Ann. §31-11-1-1 (2011)	X	X
Iowa	Iowa Code §595.2 (2011)	X[d]	
Kansas*	Kan. Stat. Ann. §23-101 (2011)	X	
Kentucky	Ky. Rev. Stat. Ann. §402.020 (2012)		X
Louisiana	La. Civ. Code Ann. art. 86 (2012)	X	
Maine	Me. Rev. Stat. Ann. tit. 19-A, §701 (2011)	X[e]	
Maryland	Md. Code Ann. Fam. Law §2-201 (2011)	X	
Massachusetts	Judicial Interpretation	X[f]	
Michigan	Mich. Comp. Laws Serv. §551.1 (2012)	X	X
Minnesota	Minn. Stat. §517.01 (2011)	X	
Mississippi	Miss. Code Ann. §93-1-1 (2011)		X
Missouri*	Mo. Rev. Stat. §451.022 (2011)		X
Montana	Mont. Code Ann. §40-1-103 (2011)	X	
Nebraska	Neb. Const. Art. I, §29 (2011)		X
Nevada	Nev. Rev. Stat. Ann. §122.020 (2011)	X	
New Hampshire	N.H. Rev. Stat. Ann. §457:2 (2012)	X[g]	X
New Jersey	Judicial Interpretation	X[h]	
New Mexico	N.M. Stat. Ann. §40-1-1 (2011)	X[i]	
New York	Judicial Interpretation	X[j]	
North Carolina	N.C. Gen. Stat. §51-1.2 (2011)		X
North Dakota	N.D. Cent. Code §14-03-01 (2011)	X	
Ohio*	Ohio Rev. Code Ann. §3101.01 (2011)	X[k]	X
Oklahoma	Okla. Stat. tit. 43, §3.1 (2011)		X

State	Statute	Marriage Definition[a]	Non-Recognition
Oregon	Or. Rev. Stat. §106.010 (2009)	X[l]	
Pennsylvania*	23 Pa. Cons. Stat. Ann. §1704 (2011)		X
Rhode Island	R.I. Gen. Laws §§15-1-1, 15-1-2 (2012)	X[m]	
South Carolina*	S.C. Code Ann. §20-1-10 (2011)		X
South Dakota	S. D. Codified Laws §25-1-1 (2011)	X	
Tennessee*	Tenn. Code. Ann. §36-3-113 (2011)	X	
Texas	Tex. Fam. Code Ann. §2.001 (2012)	X	
Utah	Utah Code Ann. §30-1-2 (2011)		X
Vermont	Vt. Stat. Ann. tit. 15, §8 (2011)	X[n]	
Virginia	Va. Code Ann. §20-45.2 (2011)		X
Washington	Wash. Rev. Code Ann. §26.04.010 (2011)	X[o]	
West Virginia	W. Va. Code Ann. §48-2-603 (2011)		X
Wisconsin	Wis. Stat. §765.01 (2011)	X[p]	
Wyoming	Wyo. Stat. Ann. §20-1-101 (2011)	X	
Puerto Rico	P.R. Laws Ann. tit. 31, §221	X	

Notes: States in bold have constitutional amendments prohibiting same-sex marriage. States marked with an asterisk have a statute establishing same-sex unions as a violation of the state's public policy.

a. Marriage consists of a contract between one man and one woman.

b. In *In re Marriage Cases*, 183 P.3d 384 (Ca. 2008), the court held that the state's constitution guarantees the basic right to civil marriage to all individuals and couples regardless of their sexual orientation. In November 2008, voters approved a constitutional amendment which recognizes as valid marriages unions of heterosexual couples. On May 26, 2009, the court found the ban is a permissible and valid amendment under the state's constitution. *Strauss v. Horton*, 2009 WL 1444594 (Ca. May 26, 2009).

c. In *Kerrigan v. Commissioner of Public Health*, 957 A.2d 407 (Conn. 2008), the court held that laws restricting civil marriage to heterosexual couples violate the state's equal protection provision.

d. In *Varnum v. Brien*, 763 N.W. 2d 862 (Iowa 2009), the court held that laws restricting civil marriage to heterosexual couples violate the state's Equal Protection Clause.

e. On May 6, 2009, Maine's governor signed a bill legalizing same-sex marriages. However, in November 2009, voters overruled the law.

f. The Supreme Judicial Court has interpreted "marriage," within Massachusetts's statutes, "as the union of one man and one woman." *Adoption of Tammy*, 619 N.E.2d 315 (1993). However, in *Goodridge v. Dept. of Public Health*, 798 N.E.2d 941 (Mass. 2003), the court construed the term "marriage" to mean the voluntary union of two persons as spouses, to the exclusion of all others.

g. On June 4, 2009, New Hampshire's governor signed a bill legalizing same-sex marriages.

h. The New Jersey Supreme Court held that the state's constitution requires that same-sex couples be granted the same rights as married heterosexual couples. The Court left the definition of marriage to the legislature. *Lewis v. Harris*, 908 A.2d 1196 (N.J. 2006). On December 15, 2006, the legislature declined to expand the term "marriage" to include same sex couples. Instead, the legislature created a civil union status for same-sex couples effective February 2007.

i. Marriage is a civil contract requiring consent of parties.

j. Marriage has been traditionally defined as the voluntary union of one man and one woman as husband and wife. See, for example, *Fisher v. Fisher*, 250 N.Y. 313, 165 N. E. 460 (1929). A basic assumption, therefore, is that one of the two parties to the union must be male and the other must be female. On the basis of this assumption, the New York courts have consistently viewed it essential to the formation of a marriage that the parties be of opposite sexes. On June 24, 2011, New York's governor signed a bill legalizing same-sex marriages effective July 24, 2011.

k. Effective May 7, 2004.

l. Marriage is a civil contract entered into in person by males at least 17 years of age and females at least 17 years of age, who are otherwise capable, and solemnized in accordance with ORS 106.1.

m. Men are forbidden to marry kindred (§15-1-1). Women are forbidden to marry kindred (§15-1-2)

n. On April 7, 2009, Vermont became the first state to legalize same-sex marriages legislatively. State legislatures garnered a sufficient number of votes to override the governor's veto.

o. Effective June 7, 2012.

p. Marriage, so far as its validity at law is concerned, is a civil contract, to which the consent of the parties capable in law of contracting is essential, and which creates the legal status of husband and wife.

Author Contact Information

Alison M. Smith
Legislative Attorney
amsmith@crs.loc.gov, 7-6054

www.ingramcontent.com/pod-product-compliance
Lightning Source LLC
Chambersburg PA
CBHW081412170526
45166CB00010B/3307